Between the Bell Struck and the Silence

Caitlin Press Inc.
3375 Ponderosa Way
Qualicum Beach, BC V9K 2J8
www.caitlinpress.com

Text design and cover design by Sarah Corsie
Cover image by Pete Nuij (via Unsplash)
Printed in Canada

Caitlin Press Inc. acknowledges financial support from the Government of Canada and the Canada Council for the Arts, and the Province of British Columbia through the British Columbia Arts Council and the Book Publisher's Tax Credit.

Library and Archives Canada Cataloguing in Publication

Between the bell struck and the silence / poems by Pamela Porter.
Porter, Pamela, 1956- author.
Canadiana 20240335120 | ISBN 9781773861418 (softcover)
LCGFT: Poetry.
LCC PS8581.O7573 B48 2024 | DDC C811/.6—dc23

Between the Bell Struck and the Silence

poems by

Pamela Porter

CAITLIN PRESS *2024*

To my husband Rob, my rock;
and to Cecilia, Drew, and Chris
for your love and support

and in memory of Patrick Lane, 1939-2019
and Ronald Hatch, 1939-2021

"How a room, a bed and windows
become stations on a long journey"

Contents

III.

IV.

Crossing

Such sacrifice as the day had made,
and the night which drew you to itself,
a distance infinitely far. We stood

inside the dark, watching wind
pass in front of the stars. A fire set, burning,
the sparked leaves falling into the sky.

Stilled tongue, driftwood bone: what
bound you to this world?

From the day of your birth, the stars
knew you, and the moon, frail
fingernail of light, began its bending,

and bore you at last to the other world,
your books and papers left behind.

Your final breath — the precise
moment in which you were, and then
were not.

Mountain climber, cloud walker, the ship
of you sailed out of time, its compass set
for eternity.

May I never forget your face,
the light perpetual glimmered in your eye.

I.

Dust to dust

Open your hands over all you once knew. Write it in your holy book.

Morning, my horses chased each other through the field: the palomino,
the roan, the bay, cantering in the snow.

And the white-faced owl on a low branch, watching.
At the edge of the field, sun lighting the tips of the firs.
And the ravens fell silent,

and the owl, wings spread wide on a low branch,
resembled the soul of one just now leaving the earth.

And the owl floated low across the horses' backs, pushing wind
through its wings, and rose into the air.

The ravens resumed their clatter, and the chickadees
emerged from their hiding places.

A forest of towering firs: one brought down by a gust of wind
could take the house. And trunks so wide you could stretch out your arms
and fail to reach half-way-around.

And all nearby: fir, palomino, roan and bay, had heard the owl
displace the air. And the owl stretched out its formidable claws

and secured another branch, high in the stand of firs beyond the road,
great firs that had remained a hundred years or more.

Often I lay awake as the owls called each to each across the dark.
And with one cry, another answered, and drew closer.

Yet among the trees a murmur arose beneath the earth —
through roots unknown to the human ear
which would sound to us as a polished stillness,

and as the snow melted that spring, and the light lengthened,
nothing appeared out of the ordinary.

Yet on a day that sun-warmed the turning earth, came the sound
of chainsaws beyond the road. The land to be cleared for houses.

Days on end, the *buzz* and *crack*, the firs felled one by one.
The quake as the great firs crashed to the ground.
And the owls rose and flew.

I'd never spotted their nests, so high in the thick of the forest.
And no official was sent to look.

Five, six, seven fled as one, resembling the souls of those
just now leaving the earth.

Write it in your holy book. Open your hands over all you once knew.

"In this dark where the dead have come for blessing"

I am tired of patience. I have waited so long.
The fifth horse buried, and snow
rising, invisible, into the spring air.
Mud over the grave sinks further each day.
I've had it with death. Mice
leave their tunnels exposed to sun
now that the snow has died, now
that the earth has broken.
At night I look out at the moon
tangled in the bramble of trees and wonder
where you are. That night after your death
you sat in the chair in a corner
of my room and filled my head with words
and you did not ask for blessing.
There is no going back. Wind
has blown the snow away and all
who are no longer tethered to this ground.

Passage

For the suitcase opened and emptied
For the clothing unpacked
For lines written on scraps of paper and left on a desk
For the robin who carried a twig again and again to build its nest
For the three years not speaking before death arrived
For the decades and those you left behind
For the apple tree you climbed with shears in hand
For the cherry and plum blossoms you nurtured and blessed
For the piano you never heard me play
For the owl who watched from a branch of the cedar
For the pin-pricked light in the darkened room
       like the smallest of blossoms
For the album that was never made, photographs lost
       and those not taken
For the dates no one noted, no week, no month, no year
For your name called before dawn, beckoned and called,
       which only you could hear

A gathering of brief moments on earth

1.
The bells fell silent; only wind
rang in the empty towers.
The ferry's horn blared into the cloud
that brooded on the water.

2.
Some of us dreamed it before it arrived.
Waxing and waning, the moon
marked the time, the dead in the dream
summoned not by name, but by number.

3.
And the days collapsed
into a dull order
in which some remained alive,
and others embarked
on the perilous journey.

4.
Yet those of us who remained, lived
into a ruin — sirens roared for the sick,
the dying, who wandered out of their bodies
into the realms of stars.

5.
Month after month carried an undertow
of grief. Much shattered that could not
be put back together.

6.
Solitary in our solitary rooms, we spoke little,
lit signal fires and peered out to sea.

7.
From visible to invisible, the dream
awoke as dreams do, while branches slept
and nudged each other into green.

8.
And the delicate membranes
burst, and leaves unfolded as if
it were a normal spring.

9.
The cherry tree blossomed, and the apple.
And roses bloomed. By the second year
we laid stones to mark the path of the sun.

10.
And the bees remembered their labours,
and birds knit their nests, strand
by strand, and the horses found the grass,
a greening so tart it stung our eyes.

11.
And many who passed over in those days
were forgotten, who did not forget us:
their spirits entered our rooms
and watched us as we slept.

12.
The living could not fathom
that the dead spoke in language
which rose in air as minute
bursts of light.

13.
And daylight shortened, as it will,
and spiders overnight stitched their fractal
nets and gathered the dew.

14.
And in an unkempt corner the sun broke into colours.

15.
Hours we stood watching a fire
flare on the mountain, smoke
rising as the spirits of our dead
rose toward the moon's open mouth.

16.
On the path leading to the field, there
in a furrow you nearly step on a snail
lugging its house toward the underbrush.

17.
You pick up the snail and set it
in a patch of green, because the house
is infinitely delicate,
and there are years yet unfathomed
to be lived.

After

Winter lingered; the snow refused flowers.
As dawn broke, ravens' black wings
shadowed the ground.

And in the sky, an eagle, full-spread,
landed swaying on the tip
of the pine.

As if in a mirror, the pond waited
to reflect the sky, and this earthly road
stilled its dreaming.

This, the way the present dies, the past
towers over us; how a room,
a bed and windows

become stations on a long journey, vacant
but for particles of light, air, the great
ghost ships of passing clouds.

Portrait of the Artist with Claribel Alegría, 1924–2018

I'm standing on the bridge
beside her — the Señora, the poet,
as water below us sweeps
everything away — leaves,
branches, the broken, the fallen
trees. *My dead wait on every corner,*
she begins, and I want her
to know we have some things
in common: I tell her, *death
comes to life* every night for me, too.
How I wake and they
are standing beside the bed
peering down at me, and she
turns her head, sharp, quick,
and for the first time stares
right into my eyes. She sees me
now, and we have a conversation
right there on the bridge as
the water goes on churning
beneath our feet. In the distance
smoke rises from small fires
in the mountains, El Salvador,
and in the late of afternoon
I watch the lines in her face
as she speaks: *Claribel*, insisting
I call her by her Christian name,
and I tell her how, during the war,
some of us from the north slept
on the dirt floors of the poor
so that the *Junta* would not attack,
and I, *embarazada*, as anyone
in daylight could clearly see,
remember waking to the sound

of gunfire in the night. I tell her
I too am a poet, and she turns,
not only her face but her full
body shifts toward me, one hand
still on the railing, this woman
who disguised herself in life
as witch, jaguar, serpent, and I
see all her faces, one after
another, as she rustles through
her purse to pull out
the pen her father once
gave to her, and knowing perhaps
that by being dead, the pen
would no longer be of use to her,
places it into my palm. *Here*,
she says. *It's yours now.*
This is your sword.

embarazada – to be pregnant

Cloistered from the living

Cloistered from the living, invisible, unseen,
night under a blackened moon,

he travels between, lonely under the moon,
forgotten by the living, but there he is

in the chair beside my bed, forgotten, his face
a swirl of air lighting the moonless dark

like a sea captain shipwrecked by dark and gale,
the pinpricked wreckage of his face,

or by lifting a brush toward his face, splashes on
pigment, so his wife, brother, might notice him.

Everyone believes him gone: brother, wife —
not homeless entirely, but longing to be seen.

Here in the chair beside the bed, no moon.
Cloistered from the living, invisible, unseen.

"What is worn is what has lived"

The wild rose was full with winter birds
settled on the risen snow. Chickadee,
nuthatch, junco. And in another house,
your dying nearly complete. And the air
thickening with snow, but the birds remained.
How the heart closes a door so silently,
nothing disturbs the quiet.
And you stood up and entered a place.
One that had been prepared for you.
And the present fell away to the past.
And the new was a place only you could go.
Winter mornings you'd wake before dawn
and in that darkness, walked to the sea.
And in silence, in unison, the mute swans
took flight, the only sound in that moment
their wings pushing the air down and down,
as they rose out of sight. And after that, you knew
anyone could rise out of sight.

"It is the story about grief and music, where all the dancing is an escape"

In the immediate vicinity of death, the mind enters on an unaccustomed order of sensations, a region untrodden before, from which few, very few travelers have returned…Here…the pilgrim pursues his course alone, and is lost to our eye.
— *Bishop George Burgess, 1850*

I have watched the horse, the roan, turned loose, graze side by side
with the doe.

I don't believe you have a grave, nor any pine box.
And even now the wind carries you where you are to go.

The books on the shelves know what they know.

Apples, too tart for the tongue, which the horse, roan,
and the doe, pluck from the branches.

The soul weighs twenty-six grams. I could hold you in my palm.

*

It's no wonder you float in and out of dream. It's how you arrive
pale as wind, as I'm pulling flakes of hay off a bale,
when I open the window of the barn.

*

No footsteps to listen for. The chair, appearing to be empty,
is not. Though unable to see you, something in me knows
you've entered the room, you've sat down.

*

How is it possible you've returned?

I turn and find you in the rain, and the rain
falls through you.

And the rain at last broken, and the moon
raising itself to the window.

*

Fifty years — a hundred — is nothing to you now.
Big-leaf maples let go their leaves, and the ghosts of ravens,
and the ferry's horn, five times, sounds through the fog.

*

On both sides of your death the snow turned the days soundless.
The same snow that took the sorrel gelding after forty years.

There was nothing we could do but to bury him beneath the snow.
The grave a scar, scraped down to the earth.

I don't believe there is a grave for you.

*

And you wait like a chalice in the rain, and move between worlds.
The one you were tied to, and ached to leave,
the one you'd had a glimpse of and ached to arrive.

I have seen you now in darkness;
you are all shooting stars and weaving air.
You have no voice but the words you place into my mind.

*

While others believe you gone, believe you ash, wind,
I find you in the garden, autumn,
with the spirits of peonies, of lilacs, and roses.

*

Hands open, you arrived, holding nothing in your palms.
Now in darkness, I see, as minute stars circle in your face.

Chimayó

Rain is uncommon here.
In those days, roosters, then dogs
announced the dawn while Rosita's mamá
Inés baked bread outdoors in the horno
and sold the loaves on wooden tables
beside the road. And as we clambered
through the back door, were allowed
a warm slice each, and continued out
the front, where red chiles hung in ristras
on each side of the door.
For luck, for blessing.

In the turn of the road, the hills dotted
with piñon pine on every side lay
the Sanctuario, the adobe church which
has survived on the same ochre dirt
for longer than children know, and still
one bell remains in the left tower.

In wind, dry leaves scraped the road
while inside, candles flamed for the sick,
the lost. Inside the church and through
a narrow passageway lay a small room
where Rosita and Elena and I kneeled
on the stone floor, reached into the red
sand inside the pit, and rubbed it, giggling,
onto our skin.

As I said, rain is uncommon here,
the sky a jewel, and that has not changed.
To this day, anyone will tell you
the sand in the pit refills itself overnight.
A miracle they say. But the miracle
did not foresee Elena's papá dying

one night, winter, his heart seized
while shoveling the snow. Since
that time they lived on bundles of sage
her mamá tied together and sold beside the road.

But I will tell you a mystery: Elena's papá
arrived each night to her bed and only she
could see him. Each night when the deep
of the sky fell, if she had not given in to sleep,
her papá was there, standing beside her bed,
saying, he will bring money to her mamá,
they will no longer suffer in poverty.
Who knows how long it would take
her papá to bring money from heaven?
Morning after morning she told her mamá
about the visits. Evening after evening
the sun slipped behind the mountains
and they went to bed poor.

Who am I to say what is a miracle?
The priests from the Sanctuario finally
told the newspaper that the sand
got trucked in each week from a distant
valley. To this day, people come from
far away, and some walk, and still
they leave their casts and crutches there.

And at dawn the roosters crow
and the dogs bark which makes
the roosters crow while the Sanctuario,
the sand and the piñon-dotted hills
just stand there, and Chimayó
is the same village as when we
were girls, and just as it lives in me,
if you had grown up there it would live
now inside you, miracle or no,
carried in the basket of your chest.

Nothing as it should be

I arrive there in cold January, to find my mother, though as if in a dream in which
nothing is as it should be, it isn't January but June, Texas, the temperature a few
degrees under 100, so it was a good thing that some spirit or a hunch told me to
buy a dress, and I bought the very dress on the mannequin in the store window
because it had patches of peach which my mother said was becoming for my
complexion, but also with stabs of black I thought suitable for her funeral. And
the day I arrived with my husband and children — thank god I didn't come
half-way across the continent by myself — and even as I arrived to the church
and walked down the aisle, not to be married, but so that everyone could turn
and get a good look at the recalcitrant daughter who refused to visit or to answer
calls from her father who wouldn't stop ringing the phone until my husband's
deep baritone got him listening for once and bought me some distance, some
space in which all the diminishments my mother swept like a dust-rag through
my life rang clear across the atmosphere, and once we stepped into the funeral
parlour I stood there in the reception line with my sister and her wife who were
pleasant, though my mother's friends took frequent glances at me and said to
each other, "She was so sweet..." and though I was too terrified to cross the room
and look into the face in the casket, I did, while holding my husband's hand,
and my sister's wife mentioned the time the nurses finally, after all they'd been
through with her, put her on meds, and she said, *Remember? How she wasn't so
mean after that?* But that was years, years after I'd left home, when it really didn't
matter anymore because by then, my father had forgotten everything except my
face, though he mistook our son with his lovely, waist-length, blond curls for a
granddaughter and introduced the rest of us to another resident as "some friends
who just came back from Japan."

II.

Wheat Field with Crows, 1890

Vincent Van Gogh

Light, and the reverse of light. And the sky dark as a breaking
sea, a storm built one upon another.

And wheat bending in the wind as though alive, alight
as if it were a fire set, in search of the one lost.

Such is the wind's sadness. A kind of church
which sanctifies colour, the angelic flock of the dark-winged.

And throughout, a snake of green, a river, as though
it flowed as veins in the souls of the dispossessed.

Here he stood in his silent world.

He slapped on impasto straight from the tube.
Crows tossed in as though they were shards broken off
from the night.

Each thick stroke as if God himself had proclaimed it.

And light, the remaining light an ache inside the brain —

this the field he blessed and by which he was blessed, freed
from the cement room in which he was kept,

from which he wrote his letters to Theo: *Through the iron-barred
window I see a square field of wheat, and above, the morning
sun in all its glory...*

The heart's labour. Where this earthly journey begins
and where it ends.

"Finding what he can of his own way home"

Grand Canyon, Arizona

There is a precision in nature.
The way air is a living thing. Taking form,
changing form. Like the spirit when it has left the body.
As though the walls of this canyon were cut
with the sharpest of tools. Wind. Sand.
Olga, my mule, prefers to walk on the brick wall
that holds the trail in place.
Beyond the wall, the canyon.
At its deepest point, the river. The body
must go with the mule. The mind must trust.
The day gathers to itself pigment, and the gradations
of earth. Beyond what we imagine.
The way the heart turns into itself over the intricacies
of love, and the one who has died.
We say, "Bless this man who died."
We have carried our bundles this far.
When the mules need to rest, we stop,
turn their heads out over the wall, into sky
as a mountain climber will swing from a solitary rope
in sleep. Bless this man as a raven
spreads its wings, an island in the air.
This one who died. As the spirit lifts and rises.
There is a sacredness, a gravity,
where the hour between present and past
is a point in the palm of the hand of air.
There is a bridge we cross, strung over the river.
Bless him. Who died. This man.
We have crossed the river with him
and do not know how to go back.

Small sonnet

I take the path between the trees
and leaves rain down like light
until I reach the openness.
Even before I see the horses
they've trained their ears on me,
their nickering a kind of music.
I have a field instead of a church.
Mountains and the sea's heartbeat.
I am not alone; the dead
and the living come with me.
The field and the beauty.
An owl settles onto a branch
more bare than yesterday,
the light gathered around my feet.

She sits down to write the history of rain and suddenly the wild fall into order

Take a year, fill it with grief, old bones and ash.
When he died his shadow also left the earth,
and she the one he had chosen to write the letter
giving the news, to end with the word *loss*.
There was an urgency to the night she woke into.
There are no keys when the dead arrive
and ask one to waken, write a letter to the living.
As she reached for pen, paper, it felt as though
she were tracing her hand on stone, etching
the words indelibly, as sacrament.
And the sentences fell into her brain before
he rose beyond where the earth is worn away,
beyond memory of the body, the roads travelled
without compass. In silence that was a kind of music,
in a varnish of light that had the quality
of forgiveness, and the necessity, it was
somehow miraculous that he would speak
without a mouth, then leave this world
for another. And who are they that enter us
without noise or pain, like two owls
who measure the distance between them?
And when it was done and she had written
all the words he'd placed into her mind,
a destination to which she had travelled
and could never return, not entirely, she lay
the paper down, and the pen, and closed her eyes,
he still in the room but silent, like the raven
she had seen the day before, wings spread wide,
held in air a long time, the only blackness in that sky.

"It is now and in this world that we must live"

1.
The spirits pass through walls and closed doors,
the moon's risen light falling into the room.
And a silence rose that was a kind of music.

2.
The cosmos bloomed in the sun
and water fell from the overturned clay jar
because that is what it needed to do;
it was a kind of music.

3.
For months the sky remained a hard blue shell.
And sudden, the echo of thunder.
Someone felt a drop of rain which grew
into a symphony of music.

4.
And the one who stepped out of his body,
and the owl who called in the dark
sang their own clear notes of music.

5.
What sang beneath the earth then?
And night fell to its insect sounds, its wild cries,
which those with open windows heard as music.

Considering the passage of time

The creek runs clear and cold
and the white horse whinnies
when he hears my steps on the path.
Time is different now.
Time has come its long slow way.

To this now. This present.
I rise early, as the sun reaches
through the arms of the cedars
into my window. Every morning
the same. Four, five days in a row.

I pass the tree where last summer
a cougar sharpened her claws,
shredding the trunk. You know
it's a cougar from the height.
They say a bear will do the same,
only higher.

Meanwhile, I have left a letter
on my windowsill, addressed to the moon,
which I hope she will read. I'll wait
the hours for the sun's long finishing,
then wait again for the moon, feral being,
to climb the sky with her borrowed light.

That which we cherish will leave us before long

In those days our maps faded to emptiness; our windows stared,
blind, and the doors of our houses held their mouths shut.

Many sentences began with, *when he stopped speaking*, which
sounded like the silence in the moment before snow began
to fall.

So many words for *abandoned* — despite what we'd hoped for —
a noun, proper, alive in the world. Carried instead
from whiteness to benighted whiteness, as we implored them
to remain.

Each morning the sky burst open, as the windows stared; such
brightness as erased the stars.

In those days our stories began with *No one knows why*, and
who can say how long...and ended with an eternity of absence.

It was not as it was before we were born, not at all — and by
nightfall, stars appeared as the spirits of the dead,

who travelled between worlds, who watched our chests rise and
fall as we slept.

Through branches of the cedars, the stars and all of the moon
shone that night. But there grew a silence that buried
the earth.

The spirit lives in two worlds, who beckon in mist, at the point
of crossing.

And there was in that moment the sound of a held breath
escaping.

In its own time, its own silence, invisibly, the snow rose
into the air, as the soul does when it is no longer tethered
to the body.

And rose too, the hundred hearts inside the heart,
and exchanged this world for another, carried on the night,
risen as the snow.

And in these days, our maps can tell us little more. Our
windows stare night after night waiting for the soul
of the moon,
and our doors hold their mouths shut.

Call me by my name

1.
To undo, unmask, unhear, unspeak.
I knew what I had done. And I knew
what I had not done. But I am not filled
with possibility, with arpeggios or resolution.
Something forbids me to speak.
The language of this house
is silence. And somewhere
a box of letters which were never
on paper — no ink, no smear,
no sentence fraught with meaning
folded in half. No fading. No word illegible.
Everywhere an exodus of words,
a paucity of language for defending the self,
of reparation. There was none.

2.
The heart a fearsome thing,
the armoured heart a danger.
And I fill the room with music,
my hands to the keys, the piano's heart,
harp, strings, softened hammers.
And the house no longer silent.
But words, furtive animals, remain hidden.
And shadows grow large across the yard,
but hold no language, as the tongue
that never collided with the bell, never
measured the distance between
the bell struck and the silence.
And the cold moon answers
with a colder question: *What
will stem your hunger?*

3.
It is an old story from childhood,
but now the ending is changed, words
erased, rewritten. And the muted sound
of a piano behind high windows.
I placed my faith in the elegance
of the minor keys, which left not
even an echo in the pure silence
of the final chord.

4.
I sang to you in your last days.
The hospital would not let me in.
But sang in the car in the dark
and waited for the air,
as though it were your hand,
to brush my face.

5.
It is an honour to sit with the dying,
a stranger said to me. His eyes
were not of this world.

Now I keep watch over flowers
in their vase, the moon
as she wastes away,
the quiet death of the rain.

6.
There are no bones inside the heart.
How then does it break?

Between worlds

I spotted a tiny spider on the bedroom floor.
So small it was that I was not afraid. And tried
to gather it in my palm, release it outside.
So lithe, so quick, it evaded me each time,
and took three tries before I let it go at last
on the porch in the morning sun.
I was careful because I thought you might
be watching. How surprised I am at your visits,
the nights so quiet I hear tree frogs sing as I
search for the moon rising behind the firs.
I sleep and wake and find in the early hours
the air moving and billowing in the empty chair,
minute stars floating upward, and ask in my mind
if it is you. Before I finish the question,
the word yes arrives in my mind. I have come
to believe you are there, wanting to amend
the past; I ponder how you travel between
your world and mine, if the stars form their own
constellations in your sky, if owls
call there at dusk and do the tree frogs too
come alive in chorus where you live now,
and is poetry breathing in you still, and how
was it when they took you in and welcomed you,
and did you drop your old life behind as if
it were a matter of changing from old clothes
into new, fresh and bright as ten o'clock
on a summer morning.

Visitation

You tell me how you sat up and stepped out of your body,
were taken through a kind of passageway, and there
given a house to live in, small but tidy, with a garden.
How the garden pleases you.
You tell me you made dinner for your father,
mother, your brothers, that they are all looking well.
You look back on the long season of your life,
what you believed then, the certainties you kept
or threw away, and speak of your blindness,
the mountain of regrets — how sorry you are
over many things, how content with your success.
I listen as you put words in my head
for all that your hands made holy, all you vow
to make right with the living, as you turn over
one stone at a time, examine each in the light,
lifted from the waters of remembering.
What was lost, what saved, stuffed into your pockets.
The love you withheld from those who loved you.
And with an air of breathlessness, you recall again the way
you rose before dawn, and took your first steps toward the new
buds filling the branches, frail, delicate, and raw.

Elegy

Beyond the familiar, without a bed to lie in,
without a table for eating. A fire
burned down, burned to the soil.
But the heart lives, even without its muscle,
breathes what claims it, whom it claims.
The heart held. I carry him now
who cannot carry himself.
There is a quiet now, like water, the heart held,
the way water fits itself to the vessel,
a boat to travel across loneliness,
a lake where trees lean over the water.
And travel beneath, or over. At night
I lie down as he lies down, whom no one can see,
but grasp the silence in my fists, the mouth
singing, the heart a bell as fierce as its ringing,
another kind of light to begin the day.
I hold to myself all I remember of you.

You understood the way you would go

Stone paths in the garden.
Rhododendron
in bloom.
The cat slips
delicately
beneath the gate
and is gone.

That was you.

There is a holiness we carry,
we take with us.

Sun setting
and the moon in its rising
light the scattered
pebbles
you slip past along the way.

Nevertheless

It was important that the soaked earth dry,
day after slow day, the world greening
and the four horses in the field.
She never understood why he held his heart
tight as a fist, locked up for fear of what
could slip inside if the soft animal
of her shyness might burrow in and stay.
He'd built a room around himself, kept
the key in his pocket, a model of moderation
and reason. But she with her outsized soul
confused everything. When all else failed
he accused her of premeditation,
and chased her off. For years after that
she lay in bed each night and morning
asking herself if she had really done
all the terrible things he claimed.
It was important that year, that the snow
thaw silently, that the earth remain steadfast
in its tilt toward the sun, that his ashes drift
bird-like over the river. And the field
continued its greening, and the four horses,
and the one wild tree that once a year
burst its delicate flowers.

The Sower

Vincent Van Gogh

How it begins: a piece of white paper, a blank canvas.
The sun at its zenith, poplars on a hill,
                                        blazing.
And at sunset, a gleaming field of wheat.

Even darkness drew him to the light.

Released from the asylum to live near Dr. Gachet,
he painted.

He piled his work in a sort of hovel where goats
were usually kept. Every day he brought new ones in —
no one ever looked at them...

Both sower and reaper.
His shoes, tossed onto the floor, swallowed
the darkness,
                    shone back the light.

In Saint-Remy, his *Road with Cypresses* left behind,
hung on a chicken coop gate.

And where is the night in which all things are mended,
and where is the dawn in which the light is reborn?

Vincent, this world takes its own time:
Life is for sowing; the harvest is not here.

III.

Canticle: on the nature of daylight

It's the tree
the stars find first
                    — Lorna Crozier, "Spirit Tree"

Light, first to be created.
Darkness our eternity, our birth waters.

Moon our mirror: on the water,
on mountains snow-covered,
                    and its twin, the snowy owl.

Moon on a branch of the maple.

How the days wax and wane.
As winter falls away, evening
waxes, and also morning.

When I go to feed the horses
the pasture gate is in the near.
The horses graze in the far.

            After the winter's rain
there's the smell of rotted wood
and mud, and slumped piles of manure
as the horses
raise their heads and whinny.

And the life breaks open, as it did
at the world's birth.
                    And in the far,
a cluster of trees in early sun,
their branches naked and the sap red,
fire red and flaring.

                    — after Max Richter

In answer to your question

Do you know the wild horse poem?
The sound of unshod hooves on desert grass, running?
— *Patrick Lane*

Now is the time of the wild horses.
Their hoof prints in soil beget the lines of the poem
never written, but for the cuneiform left in dust.
Lines we were powerless to decipher, though we knelt
in the sand, studied them like scholars.
How we rode straight up and straight down
the scree slopes in wind. Sand in our eyes.
The heave of their rumps and the rising of the forelegs
as they pitched forward, upward.
Instinct it was, alive in them, the wild inside.
Another mountain and the route plunging down,
the tough little apples we plucked, held flat on our palms,
which, eager, they took with their teeth and scraped our skin,
the way you held birdseed in your hand stretched high,
and the birds would come. And we, unimportant,
the parched creek beds winding, the horses guided by instinct
and the jays' startled blue overhead.
The snort from their nostrils when we started up slope again.
There is wild in every horse.
Even if you are riding its back, saddled or bare.
Yes, I know the wild horse poem.
But there is more than one. Which one do you know?

There is a silence

There is a silence in forgiving,
the way a stone is dropped
into a well, as water
slips it into its mouth
with such quiet,
the ear cannot detect it.
The light does not know
it turns the colour of the leaves.
Silence does not feel its own weight.
I believe that to listen
is better than to speak,
like the heart's ear that hears
the slightest singing.
The engine of the heart
that knows I was loved, even if
for years we did not speak.
The heft of such silence
balanced against the light,
and shadows that move over
the field and the barn's open door
from morning into night.

For the first time

There is singing the way the stars would sing
if you could hear them. The sound of a choir.
What you hear is silence, but the singing is there,
in the place where the unknown is born,
though what you can see are the hills, blacker than night,
and the constellations writing their stories
who give birth to music as a whale births her calf,
the deer her fawns, a stem her leaves. All singing.
The darkness is made lighter by the beauty.
Struggle and failure is the birth of a new thing in us.
Then one day you wake, and the trees have blossomed,
and if you look into the night, you notice for the first time
the galaxy tended carefully by a woman planting flowers,
her cold breath circling around and around her.

Dvořák in the New World

The past has its own terrible inevitability.
But it is never too late to change the future.
— Heather Cox Richardson

When Antonín arrived by train that summer to Iowa, a day's travel away in South Dakota, the Lakota Sioux leader Sitanka already had pleaded for his people to surrender to the soldiers searching for them. Sitanka, weak with pneumonia. His people without food, exhausted, cold. All agreed to surrender, be marched to a camp on Wounded Knee creek. By then, Sitanka, so ill he could not sit up. His nose dripping blood. Soldiers lifted him into a wagon, and the remainder of the band shuffled behind. A year or two after, Dvořák entertained with organ recitals in the little Bohemian church in Spillville. He'd just completed his Symphony for the New World, filled with American melodies tucked into the work. Sitanka and his people already had stumbled into the camp on Wounded Knee creek and bedded down. Unexpected, the Seventh Cavalry appeared and trained their guns on Sitanka and his wayworn group.

That was December 28. The next day a rifle fired into the sky without intention, and over the next two hours the soldiers hunted down and slaughtered hundreds: men, women, children. In December, Dvořák travelled to New York to premiere his symphony, using African American and Native American melodies introduced to him by his student, Walter Burleigh, though later he insisted that all the melodies in the symphony were his own.

Unaccompanied Minor

Menor no acompañado

Mamá sent me, her only son, with some
others from our village, and warned
if I stayed I'd be killed, or sucked
into a gang. We walked so long
we lost count of the days. Others
fell back, searched in Chiapas for land.

I walked on alone. *Demasiado* hunger.
Demasiado thirst. And fell sick from
the water, dizzy from too little sleep.
Cooked rats if I could make a fire.
Stole chicken eggs and swallowed
them raw. And stumbled finally onto

a city of people sitting on the ground.
See that wall? they said. *Los Estados Unidos —*
and waved an arm. Some with food
gave me what they could. And a border
official picked me out from the crowd,
stared down on me.

Name? *Horacio.* Age? *Quince — Fifteen.*
Country? *Honduras.*
And for some moments looked hard
at my feet. How'd you lose your shoe?
He demanded an answer.
No lo hice, le dije. Encontré este.

I didn't, I told him. *I found this one.*

Dusk

Sun going down on the water, and he, stone still,
seated on a boulder, watching sparrows veer
in the squall brooding up from the south
as an eagle stormed down the sky, its eye
and claws on a salmon, silvered, the sea
folding over the place it came from, and the bird
rising, shoving the air, great gulps of it, behind.
And he, following the sky where Orion would form,
a man with more past than future in him, the ruins
of his life inside him, the little bells in his head
ringing bright behind his eyes, as though
he climbed a set of stairs step by precise step
into a darkened room, the oil lamp empty,
                              only the wick remained.

Afterword

If there is forgiveness,
it is here on Earth that we forgive.
It is here the heart breaks
and here it mends.
Now I talk to the dead as though
they are alive still, and wonder
if they are cared for, if the light
comes raw and new each morning.
If there is morning, or if the dead
grow wild as weeds in a neglected field,
the doors off their hinges, roofs
rusted, leaking. If they answer us
when we speak. If there is love there,
if there is beauty, if the air
is perfumed by lilacs in the brief
turning of the day.

Boarding house, Auvers

Adeline Ravoux

I admit that it is difficult to say what one wants —
in the same way as you cannot paint things as you see them.
                    — Vincent Van Gogh

To this day I remember clearly all those canvasses —
he'd bring in three a day! The Auvers Town Hall,
decorated for Bastille Day; those thatched cottages
at the edge of town, as though that were a decent
subject for art; oh, and the church in Auvers, and on
and on. The first time Father saw one of Vincent's
canvasses under the stairs, drying, he blurted out,
"Who is the pig that did that?" And what could dear
Vincent do but reply, "It is me, sir." He painted
my two-year-old sister holding an orange — how
gentle he was with her! He painted Marguerite
at the piano. He painted her father, Dr. Gachet.
And he painted me. I didn't much like my painting.
To my eyes, it scarcely looked like me, though
much later, a man who stayed at our boarding house
studied my portrait and remarked that Vincent
had divined not the young girl I was, thirteen,
but the woman I would become. I'd see him out
around the town with his easel and his tubes of colour.
I'd place his dinner in front of him at the long table,
his lopped-off ear the very thing that stood out —
but to behold all of that colour — surrounding him
in the artist's room where they laid him out,
it seemed every corner of Auvers — the cottages,
the trees, the church, that field of wheat, and those crows —
every last house or hill, cypress or bush, was alive.

To Vincent, everything moved. Including the sky.
I still have that image of him in my mind, after
all these years. There he sat, at the dinner table
with his cut-off ear, and those bewildered eyes.

"A secret more delicate than memory holds"

You will have to stand in a field,
the outstretched earth, and be forgotten.
What you have written gone without recognition.
Here, far from town where no one comes
to visit, wind drives down the tallest firs,
threatening the house, felling the lines.
It is a journey you must take: crumble
paper for a pitiable fire, smoke rising
white as bone, and struggle to comprehend
how this moment is important,
the place where your spirit lives.
What will sing beneath the earth then?
And the day goes early down to dark,
your skin lit by the moon, creases
carved by its sharp stone tool.
Given to a knowing unseen
by the human world, you grow
more feral by the day. The gradual
wearing away leaves you more spirit
than flesh, your spine a curved road
to the sky, an ending in which is hidden
a beginning. Now with patience
you've learned the air's quick gestures
in the dark, a music without sound
which only you and the farthest stars can hear.

Doing what I could

It was the one in robes, resplendent, standing
behind me, who held out the key for me to take,
and I took it — the weight, the iron of it,
unlocked the wooden door in his chest
and pulled it open, rounded to a point at the top
where inside, I found the heart wrapped
in barbed wire. Painstakingly and with great care,
I lifted the wire, unbound the heart and found
that it lay punctured where the barbs had pierced
the soft flesh of the muscle. As I worked,
the one in robes, who neither spoke nor made
any utterance at all, handed me a cup into which
I dipped my fingers, then rubbed the salve
meticulously into each wound. And one by one,
the birds returned and perched on the leafy branches
which shaded the heart. And down in the valley,
deep inside the chest, the land fertile, green,
as the birds built their nests and sang, and deer
grazed, and the sun was either rising or setting,
though all shone as gold. Then I closed
the heavy door, turned the lock and handed
the key to the one in white, who slipped it
into a pocket which appeared to vanish
together with the key. This I did many times,
and after, closed my eyes in the dark room
and slept.

If life wants me, let her come

Never mind how we got here.
I am in my chair by the window.
I am hauling buckets of feed over snow
to the barn. Writing words on paper
torn from a sack of feed.
I will still be here, doing the same thing,
the feathered, frozen air firming
my breath at the window.
And months later, the bruised sky
falling away to sleep. And narrow
corridors carved by rain.
Darkness to light to darkness.
The visible and invisible.
The wren never thinks about
another way to live: Show
that you mean no harm. Receive
everything as seriously as dream.
I am here with one light on,
my heart high in my chest, a lamp
blazing out its flame.

If life wants me, she knows where I am.

— *after Linda Gregg*

The long road from Abiquiu

Christ in the Desert Monastery, New Mexico

Midnight and no moon, no light in the canyon.
The darkness absolute. The monks have sung
the Compline and in silence retreated each
to his spare cell and bed. And not yet four a.m.
when they will wake and shuffle over dry
grass and sand to sing the morning in. The wild
geese are bedded down, and the two blackbirds
who mated in the sky today above the cliffs.
The doe and her fawns curl together
in the underbrush. Only the river lies awake,
tumbling over rocks in its course that weaves
and bends according to the will of earth.
We travelled the arduous route, navigated
the road which, after rain, dissolved into clay.
We have faced the wind in the canyon
and the sun's stretch in striations of colour
and stone. Now night has fallen to a depth
we have never known, but for the repletion of stars
we'd been told all our lives were there,
but were blind to in the lamp-lit world.

Asylum

A grain of madness is the best of art.
                    — Vincent Van Gogh

It's always the real world, Rilke said.

Forbidden from painting in his cell, he was given
          an empty room in which to work.
When let outside, he painted road menders in the street,
                    trees in front of the asylum.

At night, through the iron bars of his window
                    he painted the moon and stars.

There is a music which passes from eye to hand, to brush.

What is the sound of moonlight?
                    Do we hear it when the owl is silent?

For the letters to Theo written each morning
                    in a voice like ripening wheat.

For the schoolboys, for the stones thrown from their hands.

For the dream, and for waking to the sound of wings.

Some of us seem always to have the face of one about to leave this world.

Somewhere a ship passes on the sea,
                    and small boats sleep, rocking on the Seine.

He could have painted it from memory: the boats,
                    and the wings of mute swans risen out of sight.

And so we live, constantly saying farewell.

Visible and invisible

Because our sight is not fully evolved,
there are colours we don't see.
We cannot then, imagine a new colour,
only combinations of the old. Like that year
I drove the canyon road every night
and had to pay attention, due to the failing light
and sudden drop at the edge.
And how close I felt to the wolf's eyes in the dark.
And what colour was the owl's song those nights,
and the sparrow's, and what do the dying see,
what the shades of grief do the living bear,
while the soul spreads its colours, as the moon does.
And the colour of silence. Of wind. The colour of rain.

IV.

The Lieutenant

He continued soldiering long after the war,
Lieutenant over two small girls.
The summer heat stood at attention, sweated
out the days and weeks as a silence hung
over the house, the girls commanded not to speak
unless spoken to. Until the younger one climbed
high in the sycamore, sealed her mouth shut
and would not open it. Words burrowed inside
her and no one to trust in the telling. Her tongue
grown sickly from neglect, she searched
for words in books which appeared instead
as little birds she imagined holding in her palm.
The air grew colder, the leaves, in salute, flew
higher, her tree buffeted by wind as salt tears
streaked her face. The sycamore her sanctuary.
It did not occur to the Lieutenant or his wife
or to the sister that the child had been blessed
with a hidden understanding of the music
in loneliness and wings, or the way the sky
deepened on the rutted road toward winter.
She read messages the leaves left for her, the size
of the Lieutenant's wide hand, her face stung
with the thought of him. Here it must be noted
also that a war raged in the house between
the Lieutenant and his wife. The elder sister
allied herself with the mother and took
on a certain degree of power as the house —
foundation, bricks and mortar, kept the battle
from neighbours on either side. As the wind
rose and the night stole in, the girl held
her grip on the tree, and even as she clung,
surrounded by bare branches, the Lieutenant
never thought to look up to find her. Yet
the chickadees, sparrows, the commonest of birds

settled in their nests beside her and breathed
from the nostril-holes in their beaks and blinked
their fine, feathered eyelids, unafraid.
And she listened to the prayers of grass and beheld
all she could of the stars she wanted to grasp
in her fist, and which still found her once
she climbed down and slipped into bed
beside her window in the dark.

"There is nothing that cannot be seen"

a passing over
a passing through
how water fits itself
into a vessel, the same water
freed and falling, a gravity
an owl calls, just there —
and pierces the night
Forgive us our longing
I remember what I can
of sleep, where the dead
go to find us, nothing
is secret from them
Who knows where things finish?
It is enough, this forest, these
firs, this rocky soil, the rains
forgiveness is a curtain
flared into a room
captured in a mirror
as ships pass, ferrying
journeyers through the strait
who wave and wave their arms
the ferries' horns sounding
as they meet and depart

The cure for tomorrow

— a spell

Take three strands of horse's tail. Braid them together.
Add the feather of a Steller's Jay.
Do this with the moon at your back.
Then turn, face the mountain.
On your knees, brush the hair of the water.
Recite the words given you in the dream, the one
in which the swans return. Soon enough,
the maple will release her hundred children.
Wait there, and watch her fill with light.
Every morning you will be given back to this world.
You do not need to understand.
Stay awake while the moon lays down her light,
delicate as designs cut into paper.
Now open your palms — there lies the map
you must decipher, the secret to your life.
Inside you a compass is hidden. It will show the way.
Put your ear to earth — listen for a beating heart.
She is still alive. Now is the time.

Standing empty-handed under the sky

The cliff face all along was the journey
and sun where the light stretched out
and the light sliding away also was the journey.
And the road into the interior. Unpaved,
impassable after rain. And the wooden gate
was there all along to be opened, to let you
through. And the owl who looked down at you
and spread its miraculous wings and flew
was the journey, and the wolf on that one day
standing alert, eyes locked with yours as though
it knew what your life was for, and the river
that ran clear, fast and cold, and the dead in spirit
who sat by your bed as you slept, all along
was the journey, was the journey all along.

Unadorned

The mother knows that the Lieutenant
does not arrive home until the dinner hour,
and the mother, too, knows that the child
will arrive late from school, will carry
the weight of a violin home.
It has been the girl's practice to drop
her books at the base of the sycamore
and climb into its branches and thereby
survey both the back and front
of the house, and yes, that car is parked
as usual, several houses down.
The man never parks the car in front
of the house. The mother once told
the girl that the man was a salesman,
that she bought nothing from him
but he returns nonetheless. Once
the child has climbed high enough
into the branches of the sycamore,
she can see clearly into her mother's
bedroom window where, at this
moment, the man is undressing
and is, simultaneously, beginning
to undress her mother, quickly,
hurriedly, and he is unbuttoning
her blouse while her mother is stepping
out of her slacks and they move onto
the bed while his mouth is on hers,
his hands on her breasts, and then
his mouth on her breasts, and he
lies over her, the blouse crumpled
beneath, and now they have turned,
the mother on top, one breast
in his mouth, and she is rocking
on top of him when, sudden, she

collapses a little, and he shudders,
and she falls onto him. And there
is a moment of calm until she points
to the clock and she gathers herself,
and frantic, dresses, and the man too,
and the child watches as he strolls
down the front steps and down the block
where she sees his car pull away.
And the child climbs down.

Harbour

Knowing what you knew then, driving north,
the traffic arrow lit green, a voice sudden
in your head — that, or some

celestial being called out, instructing
you to turn, drive up the dark
hill where the hospital lights burned low,

the night bereft of stars,
you drove in, parked the car, and though
you did not know to which hospital

they'd taken him, and unsure
if he was inside, if it was the right one,
understanding full well

it would take a miracle for you and him
to speak again,
you sat in that shadowed wilderness,

only a few cars sleeping there and all
you could do was to sing.
And you did,

windows rolled up, and sang toward
the cinderblock walls,
relentless maze of rooms,

hallway gurneys dead silent; and still
you held on, the hall of souls,
your voice as if

in a dream, a reverie —
that's what it was — a harbouring,
and singing to no one who could hear

was forgiveness, fire and ice
reconciled for once
and perhaps for all. Into the high octaves

you sang toward eternity, and the moon
veiled, a clouded brightness,
raised its face and whitened like a star.

Visitor

No one calling in the night but for
the voice of silence, the swirling air
and you, abandoned to eternity where

You live lonely, if not alone. It's why
you come to see me in the night, if only
to sit in the corner chair, watch me sleep.

Outside, the moon is almost full, the dark
whispers loud enough to open my eyes,
and there you are, a cloud of pin-pricked lights.

What can I say now of the ways I pleased
and displeased you? And here you come like clockwork,
though time for you has flown. Ask the night,

ask the sky that lies covered in blossoms
beyond the reach of the tall-dark pines.

Personal distance

I like it best before the people come out.
When the morning is delicate and shy
and it's just the horses, the dog and me.
I carry out hay in armloads
for the Mustang, the Shetland, the Welsh.
Each horse with his own grassy mound.
I show them my passion for the way
spring is bowing toward the sun,
my joy as the grasses reach toward
the barbed-wire fence, my happiness
for the winter-weary firs that did not
blow down in the storm.
I tell them how, as a child, a vacant lot
was all the wild I knew, and dreamed
the forests I read about in books.
So not to startle the new buds,
I whisper to them that I, too, am shy;
how hard it is, what effort to form the words
when someone stops along the trail to talk,
my ear listening for news the ferns have to tell,
and the mosses who cover the nurse log
with the everlasting silence of the soul.

When an owl answers the twilight

the horse and doe graze the pasture
side by side. And seeing them, the moon
opens her sleepy eye just enough
as the last light makes the grasses glow.
Always there is the sound of their breathing —
horse, doe, and moon. It is the light, thin,
that leads them like divers into the sea
of night, as spiders knot their nets,
which by dawn will hang beaded with the dew.

Like trying to see through broken glass

It is possible to be with someone who is gone.
The way they approach you as a dragonfly,
or how the lamp flickers for no reason
you can think of. You walk into a room
and they've just turned a corner, the scent
of cigarette in the air. In the book
the women get to the tomb before anyone else
and find the Christ walking among them,
a story the men dismiss.
The dead come to us, curious about our lives,
and wonder if we've gone on without them.
If the memory of things we loved includes them.
If the heart still aches because they died.

The letter

The intent unspoken, but somehow understood,
she agreed there in the night to write the letter,
which she was to take to his wife, he unsure how
to explain, but working out the words and placing them
like bouquets of flowers in her mind —
"I have not left but remain beside you...
I will be the flame in the candle, the bird at the window..."
she writing down the words for his wife who lay
in another house not sleeping, the words simple,
but not, how a life mattered, a shattering,
so that she rose from bed for pen and paper,
not startled at all, and switched on a lamp, dim,
though he had refused speaking to her for years
before this night, but going to her now, and she
needing to forgive him right then and there,
but he had come to her and not to another
but to her alone, and he knew only she could help him
at this moment, aware of his form taking up the chair
and only the outline of him, nothing more,
sitting silent there, how far away he seemed,
looking not at her, coming as he did with a need
not of the body which he abandoned a little before,
and he looking at the floor and the words
filling her head of a sudden, all crowding to get in
as she wrote, the mirror over the dresser reflecting
only the lamp, the white walls darkened by the absence
of a moon, and he in the chair in a corner of the bedroom,
four forty-four a.m.

"The silence of the dead is all we own"

That morning near dawn, I went out to the horses
as the sky brightened slowly, deliberately, as
the lead mare whinnied, and I sectioned off flakes
of hay from a bale, one for each horse — quiet,
the dawn, the sun rising in the sky and the sound
of nickering from their throats, the three eager
for hay and buckets of feed, and I saw then
that part of the fence had broken, had fallen
to the ground, and as they ate I ventured down
toward the creek where the fence wire lay beside
the underbrush where towering firs and cedars
shadowed the place where the creek ran through the field,
its water clear, cold, swift, and I felt something,
a presence, and looked up, and there stood a wolf,
dark-faced with grey at the tips of its ears, standing
beside the nurse log crumbling through time
and weather; I stopped still, held my breath, and knew
that to turn, to run, could be fatal, and so I stood
eye to eye with the wolf, how the yellows of its eyes
pierced mine; I worked to slow my breathing
and so we regarded each other: the wolf must have
arrived by swimming the strait under moonlight
when no human could catch a glimpse or run into
a house to grab a shotgun; I wanted the wolf to live
and had determined that its stare may have been
a means to communicate, but for what purpose
I did not know, and at that moment the wolf
sat back on its haunches and then lay down in the cool
dark dampness beneath the trees, and something
inside me knew: he had come in a form in which I
could see him — my father, come back as wolf.

In the days that passed, I would catch a glimpse
of him, of his eyes among the brambled underbrush
or beneath the feral apple at the edge of the wood,
his ears swivelled to one sound or another, to the sound
of my voice, and the clarity then, that this was the way
he had chosen to return.

Theology

Hidden all summer, now I can see the eagle's nest.
Now sky pours through the branches,
their slenderness among the darker firs.
They say the dead live a metre above us.
It's how I saw the figure in robes and sandals
hovering in air on an ordinary morning
as chickadees carried on with their chatter.
Some nights I wake and fall back into my body.
Some nights I wake to a face staring into my own.
Since you died, I rise from dreams in which you
won't stop calling. Now, at the edge of the wood
where all night spiders have knotted their nests,
the frangible dawn pales the sky; now the morning
makes a sound so quiet, even the stars turn to listen.

"If I could get closer to the light...
where most of it is light"

Out beyond where the earth is worn away, beyond dreams
of the body and its dark roads, lay the canyon — cliffs

striated blood and rust, and a white with the sun behind
that could blind you, the canyon a red floor, earth
taking flight in wind like hawks rising, riding thermals

higher and higher, and darkness as deep, one might say
profound — a blackness unseen in a century, lit only

by a splay of stars that, if they could make a sound,
would teem — a cloud of witnesses.
                                    It was here I lived,

and here I built my house from ruin, a small adobe:
                                    flat-roofed, two rooms,
and where, in seasons wet and dry, as clay turned
to grease, when no vehicle could manage

without sinking as if into drifts of snow;
the merest slice of shadow could trick one
                                    into believing the road firm.

And so I thought it wise to remain in my house, modest
as it was, plaster cracked along the exterior which let
the rain in on days when water fell out of the sky.

And then the night: a silence which opened beyond
understanding; the sky replete, stars,
                                    the distances unfathomable.

.   .   .   .

And dawn, when it came, brought an astonishment
as trees relinquished their leaves, flew into air
                    as though imitating the birds, and sudden,
the space between branches would fill with sky.

As I'd lie in bed, the night absolute, an utterance,
a noise rose, of such depth
I thought it must have floated up from the buried
                                    nerves of earth.
A moan, a grief.

Nevertheless, it was here I lived out my years alone
but for the spirits who long ago had declared it theirs,
and here I wrote my poems with chalk
                    on the inner walls of the house.

.   .   .   .

You can have a good life, turned away from the world.

Most Sunday afternoons the boys from the monastery
whose canyon I shared, rode their horses to visit me.

Men, they were, but boys, barely eighteen, nineteen years old.
And every race, and from everywhere.
                        Who arrived with nothing but their pain.
I felt it surge in my gut, their pain, the first day we met.

The spirits warned me to expect them;
I started up the truck and bought sweets in town.

And when they arrived on horses parched with thirst,
the boys riding bareback with only rope,
I saw them as new souls, fresh, frightened,
as earth-smoke rose into air and settled again.

And I hugged them. I hugged them all.

.   .   .   .

There are reasons some of us leave the world;
given the world, one could be justified in making
a place where one cannot easily be found.

They read what I had scratched sky-blue along the adobe
from ceiling to floor. And yes, with a ladder

                             I accomplished it.
              And the house became a poem.

.   .   .   .

Fields of scrub, sage, echo of wind, birdsong.
Days I split wood to burn in the kiva, the nights frigid cold.
Night after night I opened my eyes to see only blackness.

                    When even the silvered sage
lay without light, though the constellations hung,
                           extravagant,
the night sucked of its warmth, still
the interior walls murmured my poems in blue.

In summer, thunderstorms eclipsed the canyon —
                    lightning, growl and thunder shake.
And some days the rain vanished before reaching the earth.

And when I could not make it out for provisions
the boys came, sent by an elder monk,
to bring what of their meal was left over.

.   .   .   .

That harsh beauty:
heat, wind, snow — I loved the canyon,
and certain mornings opened my door to find
a rattlesnake curled and sunning on the step.

Here where there was almost nothing,

                      sky was everything,
the cliffs whose colour shifted through the day,
the river fast, profuse with life, a language
for which there was no translation.

With every tip of the cottonwood flamed in sun
I lived with the spirits who possessed the house,
                each with its own blind light.
As the last stretch of daylight drifted off, as rain
collected in the cistern, I drank,
and filled my every pore, and was content.

.   .   .   .

                    The monastery bell
rang each morning at three, again at seven,
and at nine. I'd wake, thinking how the boys,
sleeping in their cells, would rustle out of bed,
pull on brown robes and stumble into chapel
to chant the morning in.

Against stone, and cliffs more ancient than time,
the bell rang. A bell for noon, and later, a bell
                   as light faltered and fell.

.   .   .   .

Who dares to comb the sun's hair, or grasp
what remains of a day?
                                Then the moon
with her one bright eye crept in like an animal,
broke the blackness and lay down beside me.

And the boys arrived, and rattled loose the silence
with chatter, laughter, their curses fouling the air.
                                        And no one cared.

.   .   .   .

At dawn and dusk, coyotes sang from one end
of the canyon as another pack answered,
and thus, we slept and woke to a choir
                            praising the unkempt world.
And between dawn and dusk, a field of wild geese,
noisy and cacophonous, took flight.
And eagle and hawk hunted from the sky,
and small birds mated against that blue.

And between dusk and dawn, the spirits
within the house sat watching me sleep
and wondered at the cuneiform growing
                                    in bright blue.

.   .   .   .

And I lived those years without interference,
and wonder slept with me, and woke with me.
And I filled the walls of the house with words
                                    the colour of sky,
and my visitors were light married to shadow,
the far-flung galaxies, amazement.

In time I grew frail, and the boys put up my poems
for me. And the monks brought food for me.

And one day I sat the boys down
and told them when the time came,
                            they must bury me here.

And when the time came, they did.
And a priest brought the chalice.
And did right by me.

And the boys who were boys no longer, but men,
bowed their heads so their tears
            fell into the dust at their feet.

As my poems had birth and grew on the walls,
the adobe walls, there they remain,
                                the colour of sky.

Find them if you will, but leave them unharmed.

And some days, in the distance
rain vanishes before reaching the earth.

And in the gradual warming of a day,
a branch feels its sap rise, and in the darkness
                             a seed awakens,
and remembers its destiny.
And some days a mosaic of blown leaves
scatters the boys' secret grief and mine
                             over the meagre ground.

"What we feel most has no name"

Clarity: sunlight through tall windows and the long
black piano. But who walks by to listen, here
at the end of the road? The music flies, delicate
up the scale while a dying wind brings it down.
Sent on the air like a letter. The notes bind one
to another, and beneath each note, silence.
Robins tug worms from the soil;
an owl opens its formidable wings and rises
from a branch. There are moments when
the music's mind matches the owl's,
a language for which there is no translation
as the moon, floating higher and higher,
heals its own brokenness. And the piano
makes a sound like stars, filling all the rooms
of the house, surprising us with the vastness
we have become, even if we don't see it ourselves.
Even if it feels like grief.
If it feels like love.

A Letter to M. Roulin,
Postmaster, Arles

4 August 1890

Dear Monsieur Roulin,

I write to you as the housekeeper who looked after Vincent Van Gogh, as I understand you had a friendship with him. He spoke of you often. But I must inform you sir, that we have received sad news which is greatly distressing. Our Vincent, the artist, has died.

I know that you will be immensely grieved at this news, as are we here in Auvers. It seems he was painting *en plein air* and was shot in the stomach, the bullet lodged dangerously close to his heart. He claimed to have shot himself, although Vincent did not have access to a pistol, and none was found. His brother Theo arrived to the bedside as swiftly as was possible; however, our Vincent passed on 27 July at one o'clock in the morning.

I regret deeply that I must inform you of the sudden nature of this tragedy. I can tell you that they laid him out in the artist's room with his last canvasses surrounding him, the room filled with yellow flowers — dahlias and sunflowers — which he so loved.

Horses pulled the hearse as twenty or so artists followed, as well as his brother Theo, who could not stop sobbing, on a day of bright sunlight, in the full heat of July. They buried him in the small cemetery on the hill. Dr. Gachet stammered a few words, called him an honest man, and a great artist; he had only two goals: humanity
and art.

I can tell you, M. Roulin, it was a beautiful scene to look down under a blue sky on the valley below — fields which our Vincent might have painted marvellously with his greens and his yellows.

Please relate to all who knew him, this terrible misfortune which has befallen our Vincent.

Yours Sincerely,
Lizette

Elegy for the stars

At dawn, where do the stars go?
> *They curl up to sleep behind the silence.*

Where does the music go?
> *It folds itself beneath song.*

Does the rain sleep?
> *Yes, it dreams of flowers giving birth.*

And silence? Where does silence go?
> *It waits each moment to be reborn.*

And the spirit? Where does the spirit go
> when it has left the body?

Wait, and listen: It is closer even than your breath.

Acknowledgments

Some of the poems in this volume were originally published in the following journals and anthologies: "Dust to dust," *Worth More Standing*; "A gathering of brief moments on earth," *Juniper*; "Finding what he can of his own way home," *Montreal Poetry Prize Anthology, 2020*; "Between Worlds," "She sits down to write the history of rain and suddenly the wild fall into order," *The New Quarterly*.

"In this dark where the dead have come for blessing" is from Patrick Lane's poem "Fathers and Sons."

"What is worn is what has lived" is from Linda Gregg's poem "Winning."

"It is the story about grief and music where all the dancing is an escape" is from Patrick Lane's book *Winter, no. 35*.

"Finding what he can of his own way home" is from Patrick Lane's poem, "Apples in the Rain."

"Bless this Man who Died" is from "Fathers and Sons."

"It is now and in this world that we must live" is taken from a fortune cookie.

"The Sower" — The italicized stanza is a quotation from Anton Hirshig, a Dutch artist who lodged in the boarding house with Van Gogh in Auvers, 1890.

"Life is for sowing; the harvest is not here" is from a letter Vincent wrote to his brother Theo on February 8, 1883.

"Dvořák in the New World" — The information given in the text of the poem comes from Heather Cox Richardson's newsletter, "Letters from an American," of December 28, 2020.

"Boarding house, Auvers" — Details of Adeline Ravoux Carrie's reflections are gathered in *Van Gogh: A Retrospective* (Park Lane: New York, 1986), pages 211–212.

"A secret more delicate than memory holds" is from Linda Gregg's book *In the Middle Distance*.

"Asylum" — Lines in italics are taken from Rilke's Eighth Elegy, from the book *Duino Elegies, A New and Complete Translation*, translated by Alfred Corn.

"There is nothing that cannot be seen" — "There is nothing that cannot be seen," "Forgive us our longing," and "Who knows where things finish?" are from *Apeirogon* by Colum McCann.

"The silence of the dead is all we own" is from Patrick Lane's poem "Small Elegy for New York."

"If I could get closer to the light..." is from Linda Gregg's poem "Mother my Mother."

"Letter to M. Roulin" — Details of Van Gogh's death and burial are taken from *Van Gogh: A Retrospective*, pages 211–222.

In addition, I wish to extend my deepest gratitude to Russell Thorburn, who not only sequenced the poems in this book, but who saw a greater vision for this collection and nudged me to write half a dozen new poems during the process of putting the book together. Thank-you, Russell.

About the Author

Pamela Porter is the author of fourteen published books: eleven volumes of poetry and four books for children and young adults, including two novels in free verse. Her work has garnered numerous awards, including the Governor General's Award, and first prizes from the Canadian Author's Association, the *Malahat Review*, the Gwendolyn MacEwen Prize, *Freefall Magazine*, *PRISM International*, *Vallum* magazine, and others.